Rainforest Explorer

Greg Pyers

www.raintreepublishers.co.uk
Visit our website to find out more information about **Raintree** books.

To order:
☎ Phone 44 (0) 1865 888112
▤ Send a fax to 44 (0) 1865 314091
▣ Visit the Raintree Bookshop at **www.raintreepublishers.co.uk** to browse our catalogue and order online.

Published in 2004 by Heinemann Library
a division of Harcourt Education Australia,
18–22 Salmon Street, Port Melbourne Victoria 3207 Australia
(a division of Reed International Books Australia Pty Ltd,
ABN 70 001 002 357).
Visit the Heinemann Library website @
www.heinemannlibrary.com.au

First published in Great Britain by Raintree,
Halley Court, Jordan Hill, Oxford OX2 8EJ,
part of Harcourt Education.
Raintree is a registered trademark of Harcourt Education Ltd.

R A Reed Elsevier company

© Reed International Books Australia Pty Ltd 2004
First published in paperback in 2005

ISBN 1 74070 142 9 (hardback)
08 07 06 05 04
10 9 8 7 6 5 4 3 2 1

ISBN 1 84443 468 0 (paperback)
09 08 07 06 05
10 9 8 7 6 5 4 3 2 1

Editorial: Carmel Heron, Sandra Balonyi
Design: Stella Vassiliou, Marta White
Photo research: Legend Images, Wendy Duncan
Production: Tracey Jarrett
Map: Guy Holt
Diagram: Andy Craig & Nives Porcellato

Typeset in Officina Sans 19/23 pt
Pre-press by Digital Imaging Group (DIG)
Printed in China by WKT Company Limited

National Library of Australia Cataloguing-in-Publication data:
Pyers, Greg.
  Rainforest explorer.

  Bibliography.
  Includes index.
  For primary school students.
  ISBN 1 74070 142 9 (hardback)
  ISBN 1 84443 468 0 (paperback)

  1. Rainforest ecology – Juvenile literature. I. Title.
  (Series : Pyers, Greg. Habitat explorer).

577.54

Acknowledgements
The publisher would like to thank the following for permission to reproduce photographs:

APL/Corbis: p. 8; 21; APL/Minden: pp. 10, 11; Auscape/Erwin & Peggy Bauer: p. 4, /Tui De Roy: p. 25, /Michael Fogden: p. 17, /Joe McDonald: p. 7, Bruce Coleman Inc./John Giustina: p. 23, Victor Englebert: p. 28, Getty Images: pp. 16, 18; photolibrary.com: pp. 9, 12, 13, 14, 19, 20, 22, 24, 26, 27, 29.

Cover photograph of red-eyed leaf frog reproduced with permission of APL/Corbis/Michael & Patricia Fogden.

Every attempt has been made to trace and acknowledge copyright. Where an attempt has been unsuccessful, the publisher would be pleased to hear from the copyright owner so any omission or error can be rectified.

Contents

Any words appearing in the main text in bold, **like this**, are explained in the Glossary.

Amazon rainforest

Imagine riding in a canoe on a river, deep in the heart of the Amazon rainforest. The air is hot and steamy. All around, plants grow so thickly that the riverbanks are hidden behind curtains of leaves. Among the branches are squirrel monkeys feeding on fruit. A pair of blue and yellow macaws flies overhead in the hazy sky.

Explorer's notes

Rainforest words:
- thick
- hot
- wet
- green
- steamy.

What is a tropical rainforest?

Tropical rainforests are dense jungles that grow in the tropics, the part of the Earth near the equator. More kinds of animals and plants live in tropical rainforests than anywhere else. In a tropical rainforest there are many **habitats** – places where animals and plants live. You are about to discover many of these habitats and the animals and plants that live in them.

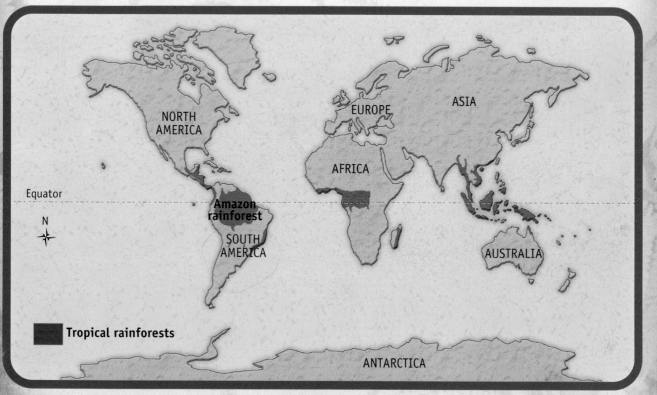

This map shows the locations of the world's tropical rainforests. The largest is the Amazon rainforest in South America.

Rainforest layers

At a bend in the river, the rainforest can be seen to have different layers. At ground level, short, leafy plants grow. Above these rise skinny **saplings** and twisting vines. Higher still are fully grown trees that may be 30 or more metres tall. Their leaves form a vast, green **canopy** over the plants below. Here and there are enormous trees that reach above all the others.

Rainforest layers

A rainforest consists of various layers, from the forest floor to the emergent trees. The saplings are the **understorey** plants. The tall trees make up the rainforest canopy. The emergent trees reach up above the canopy.

emergent trees

canopy

understorey

forest floor

Animals of the rainforest layers

Just as different plants are found in different layers, so too are different animals. Some, such as Brazilian tapirs, live only on the forest floor. These animals sniff for leaves and fallen fruits with their trunk-like nose. Others, such as black spider-monkeys, may never come down from the canopy. Many animals move from one layer to another.

The emerald tree boa moves between layers when it hunts for birds and mammals at night.

Explorer's notes

Rainforest **habitats:**
- canopy
- on the ground
- understorey
- tree trunks
- under the soil
- cracks under bark
- creeks
- puddles.

The river's current is strong. So much rain falls in the tropical rainforest that the river is almost always full with water. Millions of litres of water pass by every minute. The water is brown from carrying soil washed into it by the rain.

Soon, your canoe comes to rest among the branches overhanging the riverbank. A common iguana is disturbed. This green lizard leaps into the water and swims away. The water is calm here at the river's edge. Paw prints in the mud show where a jaguar came to the river to drink.

Explorer's notes

Rainforest river fish:
- splashing characins
- catfish
- cichlids
- piranhas
- top-minnows.

Animals of the rainforest river

Piranhas are fish with very sharp, triangular teeth. They use these to tear flesh from other fish and from animals unlucky enough to fall into the river.

The largest river animals are caimans. When they are young, these alligators hunt fish, but when they grow up, they mainly feed on dead animals.

A school of piranhas can devour a monkey in minutes.

Fish species

More than 3000 **species** of fish live in the rivers of the Amazon rainforest. One of these is the electric eel, which stuns its **prey** with an electric shock.

The rainforest floor

You step out of your canoe and walk into the rainforest. The light is dim because the leaves of the **canopy** block out almost all of the sunlight. Monkeys are howling way above in the treetops. The air is still and smells of rotting leaves and damp soil.

The rainforest floor is shaded by the leaves of the canopy above.

Down on the ground

Many kinds of **fungi** sprout from the rainforest floor. But these are just the tips of the fungi. Most of each fungus lies hidden in the soil as a huge network of spreading threads. The fungi are very important in the rainforest. Together with many kinds of insects and worms, they break down dead leaves, wood, flowers and fruit, turning them into soil and releasing **nutrients** for new plants to grow.

These cup fungi are growing on a rainforest log.

Feeding fungi

Termites scurry across the rainforest floor, gathering dead leaves to take back to their underground nests. There they feed them to a fungus, which produces a sugary food that the termites eat.

11

Animals on the floor

Some animals search the rainforest floor for food. Among the dead leaves are fallen fruits and seeds.

An animal resembling a very large, long-legged hamster appears. It is an agouti. It has a brazil nut in its front paws. The brazil nut has a very hard shell but the agouti's sharp, gnawing teeth will break through to reach the fruit inside. The agouti's sharp teeth are **adaptations** – features that help the agouti to survive.

Swimming over the rainforest floor

When the river floods each year, many fish swim over the rainforest floor to feed on the fruits that have fallen from the trees above. One of these is a catfish with a mouth large enough to gather up fruit.

Agoutis are rodents – gnawing animals that include rats and beavers.

Suddenly, the agouti stands tall, twitches its nose, then darts into the undergrowth. An ocelot has appeared. At first, this cat is almost impossible to see. Its spotted fur blends with the shadows and uneven light.

Ocelots hunt for small mammals and birds.

Explorer's notes

Agouti adaptations:
- keen sense of smell
- sharp teeth for gnawing.

Ocelot adaptations:
- spotted coat for **camouflage**
- sharp claws for climbing and holding **prey**
- large eyes for seeing in dim light.

Fallen giants

Deeper in the rainforest a giant tree has fallen, opening up a great hole in the **canopy**. Light floods the ground. All around the trunk hundreds of new plants are growing from seeds that have lain in the soil for years. Without light, these plants would be unable to grow.

Decomposing

The trunk of the fallen tree will soon rot away. This is caused by **fungi** and many kinds of insects and worms, which feed on the wood, turn the trunk into soil and release **nutrients** that the young plants will use.

This rotting log is all that remains of a 40-metre-high tree.

A plant race

Small plants quickly grow large leaves to absorb the sunlight. They then produce flowers and seeds, before the **saplings** grow above them and shade them out. The saplings grow fast, racing each other to reach the light. The slower saplings weaken and die as the light is blocked by the faster saplings. After ten years or more, just one or two of those young trees remain and the gap in the canopy is closed.

Explorer's notes

Decomposers:
- fungi
- beetles
- worms
- termites
- woodlice
- **bacteria.**

Climbers

A rope is hanging at the foot of a giant kapok tree. This will take you up into the **canopy**. You put your feet into special stirrups and begin the climb.

Many animals of the rainforest also climb into the canopy. Young boa constrictors make their way up tree trunks by pushing themselves up against bumps in the bark.

Explorer's notes

Animals on the bark:
- leaf-cutter ants
- moths
- tarantulas
- boa constrictors.

A boa constrictor is an excellent climber.

Plants

Plants also climb into the canopy. Lianas begin as seedlings on the rainforest floor. They send out **tendrils** that grasp any nearby **sapling**. As the sapling grows, so too does the liana. In a few years, the liana may reach the light above the canopy.

You stop 20 metres above the ground. Below is the dimly lit forest floor. The trunks of the canopy trees rise like columns. A flock of red and green macaws flies between them. These birds fly beneath the canopy, safe from the **predators** above.

These twisting liana stems lead up to the canopy.

Monkey ropes

At night, red uacari monkeys use the twisting stems of lianas to come to the ground to gather seeds and fruit.

In the canopy

Further up the tree, the light begins to brighten. You are now among the branches and leaves of the **canopy**.

A toucan emerges from a hollow at the broken end of a branch. This bird has just laid four white eggs inside. The hollow began to form when the end of the branch snapped off in a storm. **Fungi** entered the tree here and caused the wood to rot.

Explorer's notes

Animals that use nest hollows:
- sun conures
- scarlet macaws
- toucans
- fire-tufted barbets
- pied tamarins
  (very small monkeys).

This toucan is nesting in a tree hollow.

Mid-air ponds

There are plants sitting on the branches of the tree. These plants do not have roots that reach the ground. Instead, they collect rainwater in the little pools formed by their colourful leaves. These plants are called bromeliads and many animals make good use of them. Birds come to drink from these bromeliad pools. Frogs lay their eggs in them.

A bromeliad grips a tree trunk with special roots.

Leaves

The leaves of the **canopy** are food for many animals. One animal is hanging from a branch by claws that resemble hooks. It is a two-toed sloth. It moves so slowly that insects shelter and breed in its thick fur.

Howler monkeys live in family groups, which travel through the canopy to find their favourite leaves.

The two-toed sloth feeds on the leaves of the canopy.

Explorer's notes

Canopy description:
- light
- leafy
- tangled branches and lianas
- animals moving, feeding and calling.

Leaf adaptations

At the top of the canopy there is bright sunshine. Many leaves up here can turn themselves away from the sun to avoid drying out. Many have a thick skin that stops them from drying out.

In heavy rain, a special tip on the ends of leaves helps to drain the water away quickly. If water stayed on the leaf, mould and **algae** might begin to grow there. This would make the leaf unhealthy.

Rainforest leaves are well adapted to hot, wet conditions.

Poisonous protection

Many rainforest leaves have poisons in them to protect them against the many **species** of insects that might feed on them.

Flowers and fruits

Patches of yellow, pink and orange have appeared in the green **canopy**. These are flowers. They are brightly coloured to attract insects and birds, which come to drink the flowers' nectar, a sweet liquid. While the animals drink, **pollen** sticks to them, which they then carry to the next flower. Pollen makes fruit form, and fruit has seeds from which new trees grow.

Hummingbirds

Hummingbirds can hover in mid-air while they drink nectar through their long, tube-like tongues. They beat their wings so fast that they hum.

Black spider-monkeys feed on a wide variety of fruits in the canopy.

Fruit-eaters

Toucans are attracted to the brightly coloured fruits of figs, palms and passion plants. Their long beaks have saw-like edges, which help the birds to bite into the sweet flesh.

A family of black spider-monkeys is feeding on the fruit of a huge fig tree. The monkeys drop lots of fruit pieces. These fall to the rainforest floor, to become food for other animals.

Explorer's notes

Nectar-drinkers:
- bats
- bees
- hummingbirds
- butterflies.

Fruit-eaters:
- bats
- toucans
- iguanas
- marmosets.

Above the canopy

You have now climbed above the **canopy**. There is a breeze and a magnificent view across the rainforest. The calls of monkeys and birds are below you now.

Above you, on an enormous nest of sticks, a harpy eagle is looking through the canopy for **prey**.

Monkey hunt

The harpy eagle takes off. It is the largest eagle in the world. It has seen a monkey and now it dives for it on short wings that enable it to twist and turn among the branches. There's a squeal and a shriek. Birds scatter across the canopy as the eagle emerges with its catch. The eagle returns to its nest to feed its single chick.

Harpy eagles raise one chick at a time.

Monkey-eating eagle

The monkey-eating eagle is a huge bird of the rainforests of the Philippines. It preys on monkeys, squirrels and other small **mammals**.

Rainforest at night

Back on the rainforest floor, you prepare for the night ahead. When the sun sets, there is no light at all. You cannot see your hand in front of your face. But you can hear animals moving about. You put on night-vision goggles to see the action.

Vampire bats

Vampire bats search at night for large animals, such as tapirs. A bat cuts a tapir's skin with its sharp teeth and drinks the animal's blood.

Brazilian tapirs search at night for fruits and leaves on the rainforest floor.

Night activity

A tamandua appears. This anteater has huge claws which can rip open a termite nest. Its tongue laps up thousands of termites every night.

A potoo flutters in and out of view, catching insects from its perch on a broken branch. This large-eyed **nocturnal** bird would have spent the day sitting motionless on that same branch, keeping safe from prowling ocelots.

This tamandua is raiding a termite nest.

27

Changing rainforest

Rainforests are the world's oldest land **habitats**. The Yanomani people of Brazil have lived in the Amazon rainforest for thousands of years. They know how to hunt the animals, and how to make tools, shelters and medicines from the plants.

The Yanomani clear tiny patches of rainforest to grow food plants. They also grow plants for making poison for darts used in hunting, and plants for making rope. Eventually, the rainforest takes over and these gardens disappear.

These Yanomani men are on a monkey-hunting expedition.

Rapid change

Other people have come to the rainforest with machines. They cut down the huge trees to sell and then use the land to graze cattle. And so, the rainforest has become smaller. Today, the destruction of tropical rainforests continues to be a major **conservation** issue.

This clearing is for a village, but logging destroys vast areas of rainforests.

Explorer's notes

Why rainforests are important:
- habitats for animals
- many medicines come from rainforest plants
- rainforests affect the world's climate.

Find out for yourself

You may have the opportunity to visit a rainforest. Observe the different kinds of **habitats** you see. Observe the animals and plants you see. Perhaps you could compare different birds.

Using the Internet

Explore the Internet to find out more about rainforest habitats. Websites can change, so if the link below no longer works, don't worry. Use a kid-friendly search engine, such as www.yahooligans.com or www.internet4kids.com, and type in keywords such as 'rainforest animals', or the name of a particular rainforest animal or plant.

Website

http://www.rain-tree.com/links.htm
This website is a good site for links to all sorts of interesting rainforest websites, including sites with interactives and information on taking action to **conserve** rainforests.

Glossary

adaptation   feature of an animal or plant that helps it to survive

alga   (plural: algae) plant without roots or sap

bacteria   living things consisting of a single cell

camouflage   colours and patterns that help an animal to hide in its habitat

canopy   highest layer of leaves in a forest

conservation   looking after natural environments

fungus   (plural: fungi) mushroom or toadstool

habitat   place where an animal or a plant lives

mammal   animal that drinks its mother's milk when it is young

nocturnal   active at night

nutrient   substance that provides nourishment

pollen   powdery material produced by the male part of a flower

predator   animal that kills and eats other animals

prey   animal that is killed and eaten by other animals

sapling   young tree

species   group of living things that reproduce with each other

tendril   clinging shoot found on climbing plants

understorey   layer of plants that grows beneath the tallest trees in a forest

Index